What's Keeping You From Starting the Business God Wants You to Have?

A New Level of Faith and Belief

DezJuan Jackson

Dedication

This book is dedicated to all future entrepreneurs, business owners, and leaders. The material provided in this book is intended to motivate and inspire anyone who wants to take a leap into an amazing endeavor. Fulfillment is something often sought in life. Growing spiritually and financially can have a tremendous impact on your future. A strong personal belief in God will provide the needed confidence to exercise your faith in the area of business. Always be open-minded, and Ask, Seek, and Knock so that doors will be opened unto you! Thank you for your purchase!

Sincerely,

DezJuan Jackson
Author and Entrepreneur

Contents

Acknowledgments

Hello! Thank you for purchasing a copy of this book! I am excited to take you on a journey that's going to feed your soul and change your mindset, but most importantly, this journey will expand and grow your faith and belief system when it comes to business and entrepreneurship. Some may wonder what are the steps to starting a business or how are businesses acquired? Embarking on this path comes with many tasks and tests. As believers in Christ, we must trust Him as he directs our paths. I'm so ready to share as much as I can with you; I invite you to open your minds as well as your hearts so we can get going. The information I'm sharing in this book will allow you to see the world in a creative way while providing you access to abundant living.

Chapter 1

Creating the Vision

Chapter One

Creating the Vision

Many businesses are started with leaders who have been given a vision or desire; it's important to understand your visions and desires work together. *Vision* comes with sight, and *desire* is within the inside of one's heart or soul. In the beginning, when you are preparing for a business venture it's very important that all ideas and thoughts are written down. Habakkuk 2:2 states, "Write the vision, and make it plain upon tables, that he may run that readeth it." Vision means an experience of seeing someone or something in a dream or trance, or as a supernatural impartation once the vision is clear it then opens the mind up for desire (Oxford University Press, 2008). Desire is a strong feeling of wanting to have something or wishing for something to happen (Oxford University Press, 2008). I hope that you gain a complete understanding of these two words so that they may carry your future to abundance.

While in the creating vision phase, preparation always meets an opportunity. The best businesses have been started by one's idea or thoughts. Perhaps you have a special gift, talent, or hobby that you love or could see yourself doing every day while making a living by sharing it with others. Everyone's vision for business will be different, and that's what makes the world unique, is the variety and diversity that exist.

3

WHAT'S KEEPING YOU FROM STARTING
THE BUSINESS GOD WANTS YOU TO HAVE?

All companies, whether sole proprietors, LLC's, corporations, or small businesses, started with a vision and an action plan. Action plan is defined as a proposal strategy; a sequence of steps that must be taken, activities, time horizon to complete a task by a certain period (Oxford University Press, 2008). The purpose of the action plans is to help you understand and clarify what resources are required to reach the goal and formulate a timeline for when specific tasks must be done in order to meet a deadline. In the beginning of creating your vision for the business, it's imperative to focus on a specific need or purpose for your establishment. What will make it distinct? The definition for distinct is recognizing different in nature form something else of a similar type (Oxford University Press, 2008). A person with vision can tap into what I call Creative Instinct. Creativity comes from imagination or ideas. Instinct means - desirable one, quality impulse (Oxford University Press, 2008). Creative people generally display the following characteristics: they are bright, adaptable, have a high self-image, challenge oriented, idea-oriented, inquisitive, and curious.

While your vision is underway, it's essential to be specific about what you are after or seeking. Vision also gives you a forecast of what's ahead or at arm's reach through resources. When I created my vision for my business, I used a vision board. Vision boarding is an exercise anyone can do; I learned this method from watching business owners, movie directors, and television hosts. The purpose of a vision board is to help clarify, concentrate and maintain focus on a specific life goal. It mainly displays images that represent whatever you want to be, do or have in your life. This exercise helped me a lot! I believe everyone should create one; it helps you live years of your life with fulfillment.

Chapter 2

Developing the Entrepreneur in You

Chapter Two

Developing the Entrepreneur In You

Can you function every day without a set paycheck? Have you ever imagined yourself owning a business or multiple companies or managing people, large financial tasks, or responsibilities? Speaking from personal experience, stepping into entrepreneurship is a very large step in anyone's life. Entrepreneur development is significant. Why you may ask? Because it helps to prepare one for what's ahead or what I would call a journey of faith, referencing it to a leap. Leap is to jump or spring a long way to a great height or with force (Oxford University Press, 2008). Faith is something we can't see, but it gives the ability to trust or have confidence in someone, meaning God's promises, or something.

Characteristics of Entrepreneurs

All definitions are taken from the Oxford Pocket English Dictionary (Oxford University Press, 2008).

The following are characteristics an entrepreneur should possess:

- **Persistence:** Are you persistent? Persistence is defined as continuing to exist or endure over a prolonged period.

WHAT'S KEEPING YOU FROM STARTING THE BUSINESS GOD WANTS YOU TO HAVE?

- **Desire:** Desire for immediate feedback, or response.

- **Feedback**: Feedback is information about reactions to a product, a person's performance of a task, etc. This can be a guideline for improvement!

- **Inquisitiveness:** Do you have an inquisitive spirit? Inquisitiveness is the desire to research, asking questions, eager for knowledge, intellectually curious.

- **Drive:** Drive is one characteristic that a lot of people lack! Drive means to push, move, propel, power, urge to attain a goal, or satisfy a need.

- **Problem Solving:** Being a problem solver is a very important skill that keeps businesses open and maintains longevity in relationships which is building your future to success. Good problem-solving skills are developed over time for some. Interpersonal relationships fail and businesses fail because of poor problem-solving skills. Often this is due to either problems not being recognized and/or not dealt with appropriately. Solving a problem involves a certain amount of risk. The risk needs to be weighed up against not solving a problem. Gather needed information to correct whatever it may be, analyze the best method of options to resolve the issue making sure it's satisfying to the consumer or client once agreed upon together a resolution is made, and now it's settled.

- **Independence: Being independent** is a strong trait of many business owners and entrepreneurs. Independence means a fact or state of being independent, self-determination, freedom, self-rule.

Independent leaders must possess and display great characteristics. Independent leaders:

1. Do not work for the money alone.

2. Detect and neutralize the manipulative situations involving people.

3. Are not subject to a seductive power.

4. Think of themselves.

5. Have a strong sense of personal capability, significance, power, and influence.

6. Can work well independently.

In entrepreneurship, every day there are risks and obstacles that will cause many to want to quit or give up. My mom always instilled in me that I can do all things through Christ who strengthens me. Until this day, I believe and stand on that scripture which comes from Philippians 4:13. Often times fear will keep us from leaping; of course there will be risk involved in business ownership. You thought this was going to be easy. If it were everyone, would be doing it!

Risk is the possibility of financial loss or incur the change of unfortunate consequence by engaging. Risk scares many, but how do you know what the outcome might be if no risk is involved?

In business, as you grow you will be forced to become a calculated risk taker, referring to a chance taken after careful estimation of a probable outcome.

Steps to assist you in risk-taking:

1. Balance your situation with innovation.

2. Look for all positive outcomes and opportunities with a critical eye.

3. Stop telling yourself "no" instead say "I can" "I will."

4. Always keep an open mind, be ready to change course and speed.

Now that you understand risk-taking, look for the outcome. If you don't take the risk, how can you determine how successful you will be or not? Successful risk-taking is how new innovations have been created or developed. Risk-taking creates jobs and unexpected opportunities. Taking risk shows a considerable amount of confidence allowing you to stand out. During the risk process, we learn valuable lessons that guide us on a critical new path.

Success has never fallen in people's laps; it's something we must pursue. Dreams aren't achieved by playing it safe or getting comfortable; we must remain ambitious. Embarking in the field of risk-taking will help you overcome fear. Business ownership and fear don't mix. Real entrepreneurs are innovative and creative.

Innovative means new ideas, creative thinking, fresh and experimental.

In business, innovation will come into play with unsatisfied customers, demographic changes in society, vision, luck many imagination, so it always keeps you in expectancy.

Innovative Entrepreneurship is important because this plays a role in contributing to economic growth, job creation, poverty reduction, and can help address key social challenges.

Now that your understanding of an innovative entrepreneur has grown, it's very important to know your ideal demographic.

Demographic is defined as a statistical view of a population, generally including age, gender, income, schooling, occupation, and so on. While discovering areas of demographics for your company or organization, it's critical to know target customers to ensure the business is successful, and this helps you seek out products and services. This information plays a role in pricing, packaging, promotions, and location. It's best to scope out locations and demographics before opening the business. Demographics provide data that assist with purchasing power. Find out the degree of disposable income in the community. Disposable income is income remaining after deduction of taxes and other mandatory charges, available to be spent or saved as one wishes.

Here are several important questions to ask when collecting data:

- Are the residents owners or renters?
- What are the consumer's means of transportation? Do prospective customers in the area own vehicles, ride the bus or ride bicycles?
- Does the community consist primarily of young people still approaching their prime earning years, young professionals, empty nesters or retirees? Understanding their age range is very important.
- Did you consider family status?
- Are there lots of families in the area or are there mostly singles?

- What about leisure activities? What type of hobbies and recreational activities do people in the community participate in?

The next phase in the area of demographics is demographic segmentation. Demographic Segmentation is a common strategy when you serve customers in a particular area while your broad target audience has different preferences based on where they are located. Geographic segmentation can be used in phases of seasonal, local retailer, food or territory.

Seasonal means a particular time of year when certain products are most utilized such as coats for winter gear and swimwear for beach attire; these are often marketed to geographic segments.

Local Retailer is defined as a local discount or department store retailer that sells a variety of product categories appealing to different demographics.

Small town businesses often flood the market with radio and newspaper ads that have a broad local reach and affordable rates. Food plays a huge role in very specific geographic interest. In the United States, food that's common in the south and southeast regions are completely different than the food that's common on the east and west coast. Popular foods in the south and southeast regions consist of chicken, steak, brisket, jambalaya, crawfish, lobster, and salmon, while in the east and west coast regions they enjoy more traditional food items like burgers and pizza, so you can understand how demographics play a strong role in the success of a business.

Chapter 3

Qualities of a Great Leader: Seeking the Eagle Inside You

Chapter Three

Qualities of a Great Leader: Seeking the Eagle Inside You

Leadership as an entrepreneur is very important. Why? Because in a world full of opinions and choices strong leaders are needed. I personally believe in leadership because it provides guidance and clarity of your future while directing you as well. Leaders take on a role of responsibility to help those who need direction or someone to follow after. When selecting a leader, be very careful of your reasoning. When I select a leader or mentor to guide me, it's because I see good qualities in them that I want to strive to acquire. Deuteronomy 1:13 ESV says, "Choose for your tribes wise, understanding and experienced men and I will appoint them as your heads." Before I stepped into ownership of my salon, I went through a process of seeking out professional leaders that I admired, and I worked for them and was of assistance to them so that I could learn and master what they had to offer. I was taught by my mother and family to always strive for the best and my education and skills would take me far in life. When I prayed to God to send people in my life as leaders, He appointed them, and humbly, I followed. I began to ask for materials, books, flyers, products, processing times, techniques, etc. for my ultimate goal was the leadership role God had for me in that of salon ownership. I began to ask

God for wisdom and knowledge so that I could acquire what He had shown me in the vision process. I connected my mind, heart,, and soul. 2 Chronicles 1:10-12, says, *"Give me now wisdom and knowledge to go out and come in before this people, for who can govern this people of yours, which is so great God answered Solomon, because this was in your heart, and you have not asked possession, wealth, honor or the life those who hate you, and have not even asked long life, but have asked wisdom and knowledge for yourself that you may govern my people over whom I have made you king, wisdom and knowledge are granted to you. I will also give you riches, possessions, and honor, such as none of the kings had who were before you and none after you shall have the like."* I put this scripture in my heart as I began to take part in business workshops and conferences that would open doors or the opportunities I was seeking. Wisdom and knowledge, that take you further in life, allow Christians to tap into another world of abundant living when faith is added to it.

Everyone's leadership qualities will be different, but be sure your leaders are selected wisely. Strong leaders must have focus; it's vital to focus on major things, not minor. Confidence is an imperative leadership quality because it leads your followers to success under your wings, telling them they can and will achieve great things!

Good leaders show transparency by displaying an approachable attitude, good communication skills, and being reliable and accessible if there's a need and always open to feedback.

WHAT'S KEEPING YOU FROM STARTING THE BUSINESS GOD WANTS YOU TO HAVE?

Passion as a leader is necessary; it shows the strong feeling of enthusiasm or excitement about doing something. A leader always strives to push to do bigger, better and greater.

Are you an inspiration to someone? Of course you are! Inspiration shows followers that it's possible to achieve greatness for themselves. You may ask, how do I inspire? You inspire by showing them the process and having a willingness to help attitude. Leaders must understand patience, for patience is really important; I call it a test of your will to do or test the time committed for the desired result.

How well do you communicate? Communication is important. Good leaders can communicate for this allows people to understand your expectations and your wants and needs.

Let's discuss how an eagle's leadership qualities can help man. For years, eagles have inspired and fascinated many. Often times eagles are used to represent power, freedom and transcendence. High soaring eagles are believed to touch the face of God! Characteristics of eagles have been connected to leadership because this unique creature displays beauty, bravery, courage, honor, pride, determination and grace. When God created eagles, He gave them fine vision which leads to focus and clarity. Eagles are fearless because they never surrender to the size or strengths of their prey; a fight is a must. Successful leaders are fearless; we always face problems head-on and find a solution.

What does it mean to be tenacious? Eagles are tenacious, not easily letting go or giving up. Challenges in the life of a leader are many: unhappy customers, attitudes, financial obligations, employees, but like an eagle, a leader has the ability to change and improve their circumstances and reach for higher heights only if he faces it head-on and without running away.

Eagles are high flyers. As a leader you will become a high flyer. Eagles can fly up to an altitude of 10,000 feet, but they can swiftly land on the ground. Eagles don't mingle around with pigeons or other birds. Leaders don't hang with negative, unfilled people. Eagles seek opportunities. A great leader always looks for an opportunity to excel and go higher. Leaders help solve problems; they don't complain like birds.

Over a period of time, as a leader, it's important to pull back and recharge and regroup. Eagles are full of life and vision, but they must take a look at their life, then re-energize themselves. This process occurs at age 30, causing their physical body to deteriorate, making it difficult to survive. This is a part where you need to be resting in him. Genesis 2:2 says, "And on the seventh day God finished his work that he had done." Leaders must rest and trust in Him. Eagles are like man; we are not designed to give up. Instead, believers have to ask for restoration. Isaiah 40:31 says,

WHAT'S KEEPING YOU FROM STARTING THE BUSINESS GOD WANTS YOU TO HAVE?

"But they who wait for the Lord, shall renew their strength, they shall mount up with wings like eagles; they shall run and not be weary; they shall walk and not faint."

When we pull back as leaders and rest, God works; eagles have so many skills and qualities they must go through a metamorphosis. A **metamorphosis** is a change of physical form, structure, or substance especially by a supernatural means period (Oxford University Press, 2008). 2 Corinthians 5:17 says, "If anyone is in Christ He is a new creation, old things have passed away; behold, all things have become new."

See, as a leader we don't give up. Eagles and leaders must go through things and change to remain in authority or a figure of influence. God created this eagle to retreat at a mountaintop over a five-month period while metamorphosis happens. The eagle then knocks off its beak by banging it against rocks and plucks its feathers. Each stage forces a regrowth of removed body parts, allowing them to have life another 30-40 years.

As a leader, there are times in our lives we must reflect and take possession of our destiny. Let the good and bad experiences inspire you to push and move forward.

Can you keep up with the trend of current education? Ask yourself, what areas must I improve in? Excellent leaders are the ones that always do a "checks and balance" whether that's professional or personal. I like to use these skills in both areas. Leaders make an effort to learn things every day.

The last phase, which is very important, is how can I help my neighbor or individuals who see me as their leader? You can choose to lead others by nurturing them and always offering encouragement. Leaders direct while demonstrating how and why. Extraordinary leaders have standards of quality and motivate the team to excellence.

The nurturing process is critical because it gives a predicted outcome of what is going to be developed based on the care provided.

God equipped female eagles to develop and nurture their young by forcing them to fly at an appointed time in their life. Female eagles teach their young eagles by going high into the sky and swooping from under them so they can fall; this forces the eaglet to discover its wings.

True leaders are not bosses. Leaders grow with their people; they strive to make individuals in the company grow to their full ability. Leaders never stop giving challenges, and they never give up empowering and directing. Thessalonians 5:11 says, "Therefore encourage one another and build one another up, just as you are doing."

YOU ARE NOW A GREAT LEADER!

Chapter 4

The Process of Seed, Time, and Harvest

Chapter Four

The Process of Seed, Time, and Harvest

As your journey continues, many often neglect to understand the process of seed, time, and harvest: the concept of planting a seed. I personally understand the process because I have lived it. It's important when planting the seed that you have a clear vision of what you're after. I refer to the seed as a foundation. A **foundation** is defined as the underlying basis or principle for something also known as the starting point or where someone began period (Oxford University Press, 2008). Seeds, over time, bear fruit or a crop depending on how they are nourished or taken care of; all seeds grow by a root system. A root system is the "underground work", as I call it. As I share a few reference scriptures from Mark Chapter 4: 1-12 from the New International Version, many will acquire a complete understanding of the process.
"Again Jesus began teaching by the lake. A great crowd gathered around him so he sat down in the boat near the shore. All the multitude stayed on the share close to the water. Jesus taught the things (many) using stories. He said, Listen, a farmer went out to plant his seed while he was planting, some seed fell by the road, and the birds came and ate it up. Some

27

*seed fell on the rocky ground where there wasn't much dirt.
That seed grew fast, because the ground was not deep, but when
the sun rose, the plants dried up because of the roots not being
deep. Some other seed fell among thorny weeds, which grew and
choked the good plants. So those plants did not produce a crop.
Some other seed fell on good gourd and began to grow. It got
taller and produced a crop. Some made sixty times more and
some made a hundred times more. Then Jesus said, Let those
with ears use them and listen! Later when Jesus was alone, the
twelve apostles and others around him asked about the stories.
Jesus said you can know the secret about the Kingdom of God:
but to other people I tell using stories so that they will look and
look, but they will not learn, they will listen and listen but they
will not understand. If they did learn and understand, they
would come back to me and be forgiven."* Isaiah 6:9-10 in
the New Century Version bible reads, *"Then Jesus said
to his followers don't you understand this story? If you don't
how will you understand any story? The farmer is like a person
who plants God's message in people sometimes the teaching falls
on the road. This is like the people who hear the teaching of
God, but satan quickly comes and takes away the teaching that
was planted in the them. Others are like seeds planted on rocky
ground, they hear the teaching and quickly accept it with joy but
since they don't allow the teaching to go deep into their lives they
only keep it for a short period of time. When trouble or
persecution come because of the teaching they accepted, they
quickly give up. Others are like seeds planted among the thorny
weeds, they hear teaching, but the worries of life, the temptation
of wealth and many other evil desires keep the teaching from
growing and producing fruit in their lives. Others are like seeds
planted in the good ground. They hear the teaching and accept it
then they grow and produce fruit – sometimes thirty times more,*

WHAT'S KEEPING YOU FROM STARTING THE BUSINESS GOD WANTS YOU TO HAVE?

sixty times more, and sometimes a hundred times more. It's important to listen, everything that is hidden will be made clear and every secret thing will be made known. Let those with ears use them and listen! Think carefully about what you hear. The way you give to others is the way God will give to you, but God will give you even more. Those who do not have understanding even what they have will be taken away from them."

Now that we have an understanding of seeds in entrepreneurship, it's necessary that we broaden our seed selection before it's planted or what I call "fertilization". We can do this by gathering resources of direct businesses in our community, asking questions or networking with other fruitful or established businesses.

In business I have learned there is no instant gratification, meaning no overnight success or quick wealth. It's all in God's timing. We must trust the process while living in expectancy. Habakkuk 2:3 states, "For still the vision awaits its appointed time, it hastens to the end – it will not lie. If it seems slow, wait for it: it will surely come it will not delay." In the waiting process of God's timing, it is best to ask Him to direct you.

I personally remember starting to develop my business plan and how I wanted my salon to look from the colors, the furniture, the equipment, and the lightning fixtures. I began praying and speaking my vision into existence. I linked up with other salon owners to network and develop my team of resources. I would travel often to improve my skills or to get more professional guidance in my career field; I just always wanted to be on top of my game. I remember asking God to increase me and develop me to be a great leader and help others reach their fullest potential. I knew for me to receive what God had planned for my life, I had to exercise my faith and trust more. I remember taking (I) myself out of the equation and thinking what can I do to improve another's life or add value to them? God's timing is not our timing or when we think it should be. Often times, we as Christians think why not now? Have you asked yourself are you ready? What have you done to improve your current circumstances or to prepare for what's coming?

Another area I began to exercise my faith in is giving in tithes and offerings more. Like many, I didn't think it would open doors for me. I believe it was God testing me but also honoring my obedience to Him by exercising the same level of faith for $60 before He could bless me with $6,000. Slowly I started testing my faith to see if it would manifest in my life. I did this for a few months to a year, and I began to notice my clientele increase at my salon location, which meant more income. I soon was able to let my night and weekend job go in order to focus on my business ventures. In six months of believing and trusting, I experienced increase in a lot of areas. I knew if I hadn't trusted in God with my current situation, I would have never known the outcome. This process helped me develop my relationship with

WHAT'S KEEPING YOU FROM STARTING
THE BUSINESS GOD WANTS YOU TO HAVE?

God pertaining to my finances. God moved my business and blessed me with many clients that I'm truly grateful for to this day. I'm sharing this testimony so that you will understand God's timing. When you line up with Him and stand on His word, He will honor that.

Harvest season is the aftermath of planting seeds on good soil; it's the benefit after the period of expectancy. Harvest comes forth in our lives at the end of the assignment, or I use the term 'development time'. This process never has a set date; it's a part of the Christian walk. Harvest brings out the fruits that took time, and now you can see your dreams come true whether that's a new business, a car, a home, a vacation, or whatever you as a believer were trusting God to do for you at the appointed time that will come to pass in your life. True believers stand on faith and trust that seeds will manifest in their lives. Although I didn't understand this process, I just made up in my mind I was going to try it out. Galatians 6:9 says, "Let us not grow weary of doing good, for in due season we will reap, if we do not give up".

Chapter 5

Obedience, Consistency and Persistence

Chapter Five

Obedience, Consistency, and Persistence

This is one of my favorite chapters in this book! I'm going to share a lot to exercise your faith and open your mind.

When we embark on entrepreneurship, it's in our minds that we have no limits, and we have freedom to do what we want whenever we want, set our schedules, and work when we want; I guess you now get the point of where I'm headed. But what if you do it with purpose behind it? What if you could change someone's life or living situation or inspire them for something bigger and greater? I named this chapter Obedience, Consistency and Persistence simply because I know it's something, I at one point, lacked or was not willing to do in order to elevate to a higher level. Have you ever paid attention to how jobs or corporate America works? Each employee has a specific role or assigned duties and tasks that make the company successful and grow. Companies put people in areas where the show strength or have a number of years of experience. Experience is gained over time or by actually doing something. To gain experience, we must first follow the directions of the assignment. We can do this with obedience.

Obedience in entrepreneurship is often hard for many, including myself, because we don't want to answer to anyone or follow the directions to get the best results. Take baking a cake for example. If I want to bake a cake, and the listed ingredients on the side of the box ask for 1 ½ cups sifted flour, 1 ½ tsp. baking powder, ¼ tbp. salt, ½ cup unsalted butter, 1 cup of sugar, 2 large eggs, ½ tsp. vanilla extract, and ½ cup of whole milk, if I choose not to purchase one the ingredients needed to complete the cake, chances are it's not going to turn out the way I need it to. Now the time I spent making the cake was a complete waste of time and money because I wasn't obedient to the directions. If I would have followed the complete list and processing time, a beautiful masterpiece could have been enjoyed. Successful people are obedient to the smallest of details; often times it's because it's a part of them. Get in the habit of following instructions; they are available to make things easier.

Consistency is a learned trait; it helps us be successful at whatever mission we have set out to accomplish. Consistency in business is very important. It creates customer and brand loyalty. Whenever customers or clients are ready to shop or make a purchase, they are usually on a time crunch, have a need, or unexpected obligation. To make a business successful, people need consistency. Consistency shows an urge to win, builds trust, encourages loyalty, creates momentum, and drives engagement.

WHAT'S KEEPING YOU FROM STARTING
THE BUSINESS GOD WANTS YOU TO HAVE?

I'm going to give an example of how consistency in business works because it's as simple as one loyal customer turning into many loyal customers. Suppose I own a donut shop in Manhattan, New York, and my hours of operation are Monday through Friday, 7 AM to 5 PM. I have a full-service menu offering donuts, cinnamon rolls, coffee, and assorted pastries. The first customer enters the store, and then I greet him, "Hello, I'm Dez! How may I be of service to you today?"

"I would like your two donuts and coffee special for $5.99."

"Ok, perfect! Let me get that prepared for you." Then I proceed to ask open-ended questions while preparing the order. Good customer service wins every time. Now that the order is complete, I ask, "Is there anything else that I can get for you?"

The customer replies, "No that will be if for now. Have a good day." The next morning the customer returns to make the same purchase. Why is that? It's because I greeted him with kindness, offered him excellent service, and the customer was appreciative. Now let's do the calculated figures; if this person returns five days a week and spends $5.99 each visit, that equals $29.95 a week. If he comes over 30 days spending $5.99, that equals a profit of $179.70 per month with that one customer. WOW! Imagine if he tells four people about this incredible donut shop; my profits increase! $179.70 multiplied by four equals

$718.80. This exercise is all in the mindset of a consistent business owner, engaged in being there and working in the business every single day. Imagine it growing just by a behavior and willingness to do what's necessary to gain trust.

Now we are going to discuss persistence in your business. What is persistence? How does it affect business or life? Persistence is very important to your entrepreneur journey. Persistence means continuing firmly or obstinately in a course of action in spite of difficulty or opposition, continuing to exist or endure over a prolonged period (Oxford University Press, 2008).

I'm going to share my own experience with you so that we'll grow together when it comes to persistence. It's like a daily workout or meal plan; it's first created with steps to achieve the target goal. I learned persistence when I was ready to become a business owner. Of course, like many who desire to own a business or company, I didn't possess persistance, but I knew that God wanted this for me because of my quality leadership traits. I stand on the scripture Romans 8:28 ESV. It states, "We know that all things works for the good of those who love him who have been called according to his purpose." I then realized it was time for God to direct my path. Once I made that realization, I started making adjustments. Persistence developed me in the area of credit. Credit often scares people and causes them to feel shame and shy away from what God has for them because of mistakes or no followed consistency. I

remember calling my banks and asking them to pull
my customer credit reports, and trust me, I wasn't
pleased with the outcome. I immediately wanted to
give up or pull out of what God was showing me.
Yes, because it seemed it would never happen or was
impossible; I then asked my banker where do I start
or what action plan was needed to improve my score.
Once I gathered the needed resources, I worked on
my plan. I asked God to direct me to people that
were knowledgeable of things or had expertise in
areas I lacked. Persistence came into play by a
repeated behavior when it comes to credit. I began
calling creditors to get rid of derogatory marks, late
payments, student loan debts, etc. I began my credit
correction steps for over a period of six months to a
year. I began building relationships with creditors and
paying my bills on time and consistently. My score
began to grow over a small period of time, and so did
my confidence and faith. I started believing more and
trusting more in doing the right things. Persistence
showed me that no matter what, never, ever give up
on what you are called to do or be, no matter the
outcome or circumstances that are presented, and
always stand on God's word and trust in Him.
Hebrews 12:1-2 ESV states, "Therefore since we
surrounded by so great a cloud of witnesses, let us
also lay aside every weight an sin which clings so
closely and let us run with endurance the race that is
set before us, looking to Jesus, the founder and
perfecter of our faith who for the joy that was set

before him endured the cross, despising the shame, and is seated at the right hand of the throne of God."

Luke 11:9-10 says, "And I tell you, ask, and it will be given to you, seek and you will find: knock and it will be opened to you. For everyone who ask receives, and the one who seeks finds, the one who knocks it will be opened.

Chapter 6

Entrepreneurs Instinct

Chapter Six

Entrepreneurs Instinct

Let's discuss the entrepreneur's instinct. You might ask yourself what is that? Instinct is defined as a natural or intuitive way of acting or thinking (Oxford University Press, 2008). Over a period of time, it can become a learned behavior. Releasing the entrepreneur instinct allows individuals to perform as business people in the world. It's a willingness or "go-getter" mindset which, for many, opens doors to success. Instinct itself gives us the ability to act without second-guessing ourselves or quickly changing our minds. The process can be built by strategies or marketing fundamentals to grow confidence. Business owners use instinct to capture their target customers or potential buyers based on what they're selling or offering in the establishment. Instinct can be used when selecting inventory or goods for customers to purchase. You might say "yes" to the trendy clothes or shoes because your establishment is a trendy retail store where customers shop weekly for designer pieces or accessories to complement their look. The entrepreneur instinct kicks in by the owner having inventory available in all sizes and a variety of colors. You may ask, how would I know if would or wouldn't sell? You don't know, but the instinct inside of you made sure it was prepared for any potential buyer.

Always remember preparation meets an opportunity.

Instinct is all in the mindset. How do you see yourself running a successful business? Yes, using instinct will create risk at times. I recall trying to grow in business without any risk, but my vision was so much bigger for myself I began to yearn for more and more, so I knew I had to go through some discomfort in order to get to the next level. Don't let fear keep you from your excellence.

All things are possible to him that believeth.

Instinct gives us the will to go and move forward in any direction we choose. You might ask yourself, what is my interest? How committed am I to this job? Will people like what I am offering? Are my ideas capturing to another individual? What's my location? Who are my competitors?

When I use instinct in business, I think about others a lot. I think about the question, "What are their needs"? Let's say I own a pharmacy drug store. How can I be of service to the consumer? Disabled customers can come through the drive through without leaving their vehicle. Can customers call in prescriptions? Yes because our number is located on the window or they can find it on the Google app.

Did we exceed their expectations? Yes. How? What are our areas of improvement? What would the customer recommend? These questions allow me as the owner to use my instinct qualities to ensure customer's loyalty to the pharmacy.

Entrepreneur instinct areas should also focus on product and services offered. What are the promotions? What is the going price on the items available?

Instinct helped me develop new ideas and techniques. For others to know about my business, I used business cards and social media, and I quickly learned the process of advertisement and how important it was. This learned behavior gave me the ability to get out of my comfort zone and excel in my field of the beauty industry. Some of the things I accomplished was building my brand and business, Distinctive Dezigns The DezJuan Jackson Salon. I have professional products for hair care which consist of Argan oils, hair extensions, intensive repair masks, and ceramic flat irons. If I wouldn't have trusted my instinct, I don't believe I would have had the courage to "go" or "move" in the direction of creating my own brand of products!

As an experienced entrepreneur, your instinct will develop and grow over time. Everyone's instinct will be different. Find yours; it's on the inside of you. Pull it out!

Chapter 7

Don't Stop, Keep Going, and Stand on God's Word: Overcoming Trails and Tribulations

Chapter Seven

Don't Stop, Keep Going, and Stand on God's Word: Overcoming Trails and Tribulations

Overcoming hurdles in business is one thing that every entrepreneur has faced. In this chapter I'm going to share my personal ups and downs while I was trusting God's word. I recall the dream like it was yesterday. God gave me the vision for my salon business. I wasn't sure why the calling was so heavy, but I knew greatness awaited my future. I started my business about four years ago. Like many, I wasn't sure of the process I would be embarking on, and I just wanted to take it slow and steady. Right, don't we all?

I started off in a location in downtown Oklahoma City. I remember working from 9 am until 9pm, offering salon services Tuesday through Saturday. My schedule and clientele expanded tremendously, and I was so grateful. God grew my business into a relocation phase; I couldn't keep playing it safe with His blessings. In May of 2015, I took my first leap of faith and opened my first salon suite, Distinctive Dezigns The DezJuan Jackson Salon LLC. This establishment was my very first salon on my own. I was so excited and scared at the same time. I knew I was growing and going to the next level, and while I wasn't really sure of everything, I trusted in God and was obedient to the vision.

After I signed the documents and obtained the needed certifications, I was ready to purchase equipment and supplies. This is the area where I had to exercise faith. I really didn't know the cost for everything. I had set forth an expense budget to track expenses for the start-up cost. I had money saved up for about six months that I was willing to invest into my company.

James 1:12 says, "Blessed is the one who perseveres under trail because, having stood the test, that person will receive the crown of life that the Lord has promised to those who love him. "

I remember starting out with very little, but in my mind I was wealthy. Once I received the keys to my salon suite, it was no turning back; we must move forward. I started calling salon equipment companies to purchase dryers, chairs, televisions, etc. I was excited to decorate. I went with a double suite, enough to accommodate two stylists. It was a modern and upscale environment.

Then came the the trials and tribulations! Of course, like many, I started my business with my personal savings and money. I didn't borrow or accrue any debts at this point, but honestly at this hurdle I was financially stretched and completely broke. I had a lot of future expenses owed at different times. I wasn't sure how or where funding was going to come from.

Many business costs and operating expenses can be major and lock us in fear of not having enough to sustain. Fear keeps us in bondage or content in the place or space we are in. I knew that God's plan was what I was standing on. Many believers are scared to stretch their finances, which in reality we all have to believe more is coming.

I stood on God's word, especially Psalms 23:1-6 KJV. "The LORD is my shepherd; I shall not want. He maketh me to lie down in green pastures: he leadeth me beside the still waters. He restoreth my soul: he leadeth me in the paths of righteousness for his name's sake. Yea, though I walk through the valley of the shadow of death, I will fear no evil: for thou art with me; thy rod and thy staff they comfort me. Thou preparest a table before me in the presence of mine enemies: thou anointest my head with oil; my cup runneth over. Surely goodness and mercy shall follow me all the days of my life: and I will dwell in the house of the LORD forever."

After I placed this scripture into my soul, I stood on it and believed it every day. I asked God to guide me out of my current financial obligations and to secure my personal finances by supplying the financial needs of the business! I knew I couldn't pray and not believe or to carry the load on my own, for the word states in 1 Peter 5:7, "Casting all your care upon him; for he careth for you."

I was prepared for His voice and direction. As God guided me, I realized what He had already blessed me with: a business location and equipment. All I had to do was exercise my faith and use my abilities to create income by providing services to others. My gifts and talents could carry me far. I trusted this and continued to work, and God sent many clients, which increased my finances. I trusted that my gifts and talents could break the curse off my finances. Everyone has a special gift or talent they can use to create income for themselves and provide for their families.

A gift and talent can be in the areas of music, beauty, art, decorating, personal assistant, etc. I call gifts and talents natural God-given abilities, something that requires no effort. It just comes from within.

For me, my passion was making people beautiful on the outside as well as touching their inside with words of encouragement. In life we all have struggles and obstacles that will try to kill the vision our God has given us, but we must overcome them and be steadfast.

I remember finding the blessing in my situation; here I am with a facility with all the tools and equipment needed, and all I had to do was work my way out of financial trouble. Every day I would pray and say, "God you are my provider. Send people my way so I can be of service to them. I want to have the best reputation of a professional cosmetologist I can."

With God, there are "no limits". I recollect telling God I would sacrifice it all in order to have my business. Many might think I was foolish, but I didn't need their validation for the vision I wanted to come forth in my life. Like many believers, I didn't want to speak words of limitations because of my current circumstances. Often times people in the kingdom want to put limits on God, but they haven't trusted enough in His word or been still enough to hear the voice say "Go, Go! I will be right by your side."

I knew God had brought me far from where I used to be, so how could I doubt the Creator, the one who took seven days to make the whole world. Why doubt the creative God, the Almighty God, the one who can make the impossible possible? I'm telling you, He will do it if you trust Him. No, you don't have to be all the way perfect; God wants to show you how powerful He is.

God moved me out of financial problems many times and moved my business into prosperity. I went from making nothing, waiting on customers, praying to have customers, to an "overflow" of clientele. I'm not bragging; it's just the truth of knowing your worth and asking Him to be your provider.

I believe in God's kingdom. He is my Leader, and I listen to His voice every time. God gives man vision. So where do you see yourself in the next year? Are you going to move into God's world of abundance and prosperity? These two areas aren't just about income; they can impact any area of your life.

The time is NOW! Ready! Set GO!

Chapter 8

Your Start-up Guide for the Business that Awaits

Chapter Eight

Your Start-up Guide for the Business that Awaits

When starting a business, you must establish a business name and the legal structure that would best suit your needs and life. The business name can be anything you decide; this gives you creative thinking power. Once the business name has been created, you must register it in the state in which you plan to conduct the business. In the state of Oklahoma, you can register your business name with the Oklahoma Secretary of State or at www.sos.ok.gov. Following registration, you must complete the trade name report. The Secretary of State will communicate to you whether or not the business name is available. Once it's available you pay a fee of $25.00 for the report. For Oklahoma residents, the Secretary of State is located at 2300 N Lincoln Blvd, Room 101, State Capital Oklahoma City, OK 73105.

After you have completed the business name registration, you now have to complete your legal structure. Legal structure determines the legal definition of a business or should I say your business. The legal structure can be determined by understanding sole proprietorship. Sole proprietorship is defined as a partnership, corporation, and S corporation or LLC (Oklahoma

Department of Commerce. Business Services and Start Up Guide. 2016. www.okcommerce.gov). It's important to do your own personal research and study the advantages and disadvantages of all the legal structures before selecting one.

In the beginning of my business stage, I started with a sole proprietorship. (All structure definitions below can be found at Oklahoma Depart of Commerce. Business Services and Start Up Guide. 2016. www.okcommerce.gov.)

1. Sole Proprietorship

    This structure is the simplest and very common when first starting a business. Sole proprietorship has one owner and isn't separate from the owner, but rather the name with which owner represents to the public.

    Pros -

    ➤ Simple to organize

    ➤ Owner makes all decisions

    ➤ Minimum legal restrictions

    ➤ Owners receive all profits

    ➤ Business is easy to discontinue

    Cons -

    ➤ Owner has unlimited liability

    ➤ Owner is liable for all debts of the business

    ➤ May have difficulty raising capital

> **Liability – The owner's personal assets are at risk.**

2. General Partnership

   The agreement with one or more individuals to jointly own or share profits of a business. There are no limits.

   Pros –

   > Easy to organize

   > Greater Financial Strength than sole proprietorship

   > Combines skills and judgments with partners

   > Definite Legal Status

   > Each partner has personal interest.

   Cons –

   > Unlimited liability for each partner

   > Decision authority is divided

   > **Liability – Each Partners Personal assets are at risk.**

3. Limited Partnership

   Consists of one or more general partners and one or more limited partners. Limited partners have liability in business and no rights of management. **Liability – General partner's personal assets are at**

risk. A limited partner is liable only to the extent of his investment.

4. Corporation (C-Corp)

A corporation is formed under state and federal law. An artificial entity separate from its owners.

Corporations enjoy most of the rights and responsibilities that individuals possess, and corporations can enter into contracts, loans and borrow money, sue or be sued, hire staff and management, own assets and pay taxes.

Pros –

> ➤ Corporations may raise additional funds by selling shares.

> ➤ Corporations may deduct costs of benefits it provides to employees and staff.

> ➤ Some corporations may be able to elect treatment as an S corporations which exempt them from federal income tax on certain capital gains and passive income.

Cons –

> ➤ Cost more to organize

> ➤ Subject to state and federal controls

> ➤ Corporate profits may be subject to higher overall taxes since

government tax profits at a
corporate level and gain individual
level.

➤ **Liability – Limited to corporate assets**

➤ Personal negligence or fault

5. Sub – Chapter (S-Corp)

Structured like a corporation but taxed
like a partnership. All income and
expenses are split among shareholders
who report in on tax returns.

Liability – Refer back to corporation (C-Corp)

6. Limited Liability Company (LLC)

An LLC is a corporate structure whereby
the members of the company cannot be
held personally liable for the company's
debt or liabilities. Limited liability
companies are essentially hybrid entities
that combine characteristics or
corporations and a partnership or sole
proprietorship.

After becoming knowledgeable of these
legal structures, I selected the LLC
structure. LLC is the best option if you
are following my professional
recommendation.

Pros –

- ➤ Organized to qualify for taxation as partnership (two or more members) and a sole proprietorship (one member)

- ➤ No member is liable for debts and liabilities of another LLC member

- ➤ No limitation on what persons or type of entities maybe LLC members

- ➤ Perpetual like a corporation

- ➤ One person may qualify for LLC status

Cons –

- ➤ Tax and liability benefits vary from state to state

- ➤ May not be used by banking, insurance, or nonprofit entities

- ➤ Can elect to be treated as a corporation

- ➤ **Liability – Refer to corporation.**

Now that I have shared the business name and legal structures with you, it's best to research and study each entity carefully before making a selection.

This is a personal choice and can be overwhelming and difficult. For further guidance, contact a business advisor or attorney who can suit your needs or answer your questions.

Chapter 9

Are You Ready? Let's Create the Master Plan

Chapter Nine

Are You Ready? Let's Create the Master Plan

Many successful businesses start or create a business plan. The business plan is a map used to explain and guide a business's future objectives and strategies for achieving them. It's important that your business plan is very detailed and organized. The plan should include the nature of the business, sales, marketing, strategies, financial background, and contain a projected profit loss statement. A really good business plan can't be done overnight. In many cases, business plans can take several weeks or months to complete.

As I guide you on your business plan outline, it's important to do research and study the background of business plans and what lenders, investors, or partners are looking for in the plan itself.

Outline of the Business Plan

A business plan should contain the following information:

- Owners
- Business Name
- Address
- Telephone Number

- Fax Number
- Table of Contents

Table of Contents - The plan must have a listed table of contents. The Table of Contents should include:

☐ Executive Summary – General Company Description

☐ Products and Services

☐ Marketing Plan

☐ Operational Plan

☐ Management and Organization

☐ Personal Financial Statement - Financial Projection

☐ Start-up Expenses and Capitalization

☐ Financial Plan

☐ Supporting Documents

☐ Availability of Resources

☐ Implementation Plan

Executive Summary – The executive summary is a document produced for business purposes that summarizes a longer report or proposal.

Business Description - A business description gives readers the insight or nature of the business with sales, marketing and financial background.

WHAT'S KEEPING YOU FROM STARTING
THE BUSINESS GOD WANTS YOU TO HAVE?

Products, Services and Goods – A listed service menu would be a listed description of what's offered or being sold and the price list. I used services in my business plan because of the type of industry I'm in.

Marketing Plan - This part is important to the business plan because it gives insight of strategy to target potential customers and clients. The marketing plan provides advertisement and marketing efforts for the quarter or year. Marketing can consist of the Internet, social media, cards, flyers, billboard, etc.

Operational Plan - This is important because it gives a detailed description of the employees and management's objectives to make the goals and financial projections achievable. It's important that it states the companies' goals and resources needed to complete the task to make the business successful.

Management and Organizations - This gives everyone in your company goals and tasks according to their positions and qualifications. Qualifications can consist of skills, education and years of experience.

Organization – This is how everything is set up and placed in categories. Categories can be legal structures, duties, responsibilities and experiences.

Example of Organizational File:

☐ Educational Background

☐ Employment History

☐ Compensation

☐   Record Keeping

Personal Financial Statement – The personal financial statement is a spreadsheet outlining your financial position. This document gives a complete breakdown of what's coming in and what's going out. Personal financial statements show assets and liabilities.

Financial Projections and Forecast - Financial projections are very important and must be included in the plan. A lot of projections are done with a three-year forecast. The purpose of these documents is to show cost and expenses and where profits can be potentially gained. Good financial projections have a sales forecast. You can create this document with a spreadsheet and expense report.

Capitalization - It's the cost to acquire an asset or expense over the period it was started. In accounting and finance, capitalization is the total of the company or business stocks long-term debt and retained profits.

Listed examples are:

☐   Furniture

☐   Equipment

☐   Marketing Utensils

☐   Products

Financial Plan - This plan is comparable to financial projections and forecast, but instead of a prediction, it determines how the company will afford to achieve its strategic goals and objectives.

Be sure it includes:

- ☐ Income Statement
- ☐ Balance Sheet
- ☐ Cash Flow Statement

Often times potential business owners can contact a CPA or financial advisor to get a profit and loss statement that summarizes your company's revenue and expenses.

Supporting Documents - These documents support the legal way of conducting business, these include:

- ☐ Selected Business Entity
- ☐ Articles of Organization
- ☐ A Completed Business Plan
- ☐ Cash Flow Statement
- ☐ Balance Sheet
- ☐ Resumes of Owners, Partners and Investors
- ☐ Resumes and Letters of Professional Credibility
- ☐ Licenses and Permits

Availability of Resources – Resources can be described as vendors, suppliers, distributors, lending institutions, etc. These help the business flow naturally.

The final phase of the business plan outline is the implementation plan.

Implementation Plan – The implementation plan is the process that turns goals and strategies into reality. Many large companies use this plan to give tasks and assignments to employees and management. This gives a clear vision of what's needed from each person to drive success. Put It In Motion = Drive!

I hope the material and wisdom provided in this book has helped develop the confidence and trust needed for the success of your business. Always be willing to grow and aim high. All things are possible to him who believeth.

Chapter 10

Resources for Your Business

Chapter Ten

Resources for Your Business

Each state has requirements for starting and operating a business. The information needed to start a business can be obtained from the Office of the Secretary of the State for your state. The IRS provides a list of the state government websites at www.irs.gov/businesses/small-businesses-self-employed/state-government-websites.

This chapter contains information from the Oklahoma Office of the Secretary of the State. The following pages provide the forms needed to establish a business in the state of Oklahoma.

PROCEDURES FOR ORGANIZING
AN OKLAHOMA LIMITED LIABILITY COMPANY

This information is intended as an aid to organizing an Oklahoma limited liability company pursuant to the provisions of Title 18, Section 2004 of the Oklahoma Statutes. **PLEASE CONSULT THE STATUTES CAREFULLY.**

❖ It may be to your benefit to contact the **INTERNAL REVENUE SERVICE** concerning federal tax requirements prior to filing with the Secretary of State.

FILING PROCEDURES:

1. **Prepare** and **file** with the Secretary of State one signed copy of the articles of organization.

2. **Pay** to the Secretary of State a **filing fee** of **$100.00.** (Title 18, Sec. 2055)

3. Make checks, cashier's checks, or money orders payable to the Oklahoma Secretary of State. Instruments may be mailed, delivered in person, or filed on-line at www.sos.ok.gov. The address of the Secretary of State is 421 N.W. 13th, Suite 210, Oklahoma City, Oklahoma 73103. If delivered in person, there will be an additional Twenty-five Dollar ($25.00) fee for each document filed same day. The Secretary of State accepts Visa, Discover, MasterCard, or American Express if filing in person, or on-line; however, there will be a four percent (4%) service charge added for the use of a credit card. (Title 18, Section 1142)

INSTRUCTIONS FOR PREPARING THE ARTICLES OF ORGANIZATION:

1. **NAME** – The name of the limited liability company. The name **SHALL** contain either the words **limited liability company** or **limited company** or the abbreviations **LLC, LC, L.L.C.** or **L.C.** The word limited may be abbreviated as Ltd. and the word company may be abbreviated as Co. (Title 18, Sec. 2008)

❖ The name shall be such as to distinguish it upon the records in the office of the Secretary of State from the names of: (1) corporations, both domestic and foreign, then existing or which have existed at any time during the preceding three (3) years; or (2) then existing domestic and foreign limited partnerships; or (3) then existing domestic and foreign limited liability companies; or (4) trade names or fictitious names; or (5) corporate, limited partnership or limited liability company names reserved with the Secretary of State.

❖ The **AVAILABILITY** of a name can be checked in advance by telephoning the Secretary of State at **(405) 522-2520**, checking on-line at www.sos.ok.gov, or by coming in person. Prior to organizing a limited liability company, a name may be **reserved** for a period of **sixty (60) days** by filing a Name Reservation application and paying a **fee** of **ten dollars ($10.00)**. (Title 18, Section 2009)

(SOS FORM 0074-07/12)

WHAT'S KEEPING YOU FROM STARTING
THE BUSINESS GOD WANTS YOU TO HAVE?

2. **PRINCIPAL PLACE OF BUSINESS** – The street address of the company's principal place of business, wherever located. P.O. Boxes are **not** acceptable.

3. **E-MAIL ADDRESS** – The e-mail address of the company's primary contact for the registered business. Every domestic and foreign limited liability company registered to do business in Oklahoma shall file an annual certificate each year on the company's anniversary date, which confirms it is an active business and includes its principal place of business address and e-mail address, and shall pay an annual certificate fee of twenty-five dollars ($25.00). (Title 18, Section 2055.2) Notice of this annual certificate will **ONLY** be sent to the limited liability company at its last known electronic mail address of record.

4. **REGISTERED AGENT AND REGISTERED OFFICE** – The name and street address of the registered agent in the state of **Oklahoma**. The registered agent accepts service of process in the event of a lawsuit against the limited liability company. **Every** limited liability company **must** continuously maintain a registered agent and registered office in Oklahoma. The registered agent for service of process must be the domestic limited liability company itself, an individual resident of this state, or a domestic or qualified foreign corporation, limited liability company or limited partnership. Each registered agent shall maintain a business office identical with the registered office which is open during regular business hours to accept service of process and otherwise perform the functions of a registered agent. (Title 18, Section 2010) The registered office address must be a street address. P.O. Boxes are **not** acceptable.

5. **TERM OF EXISTENCE** – The term of existence is how long the company will remain **active** or in existence for. You may state either perpetual, a set number of years, or a future effective expiration date. Perpetual means continuous.

6. **EXECUTION** – At least one person, who may or may not be a member of the limited liability company, **must** sign the articles of organization. The person who signs is not required to be a member of the limited liability company; however, this does not exclude him/her from being so.

❖ One or more persons may form a limited liability company. **"Person"** is defined as an individual, a general partnership, a limited partnership, a limited liability company, a trust, an estate, an association, a corporation or any other legal or commercial entity. (Title 18, Sec. 2004)

(SOS FORM 0074-07/12)

DEZJUAN JACKSON

ARTICLES OF ORGANIZATION
(Oklahoma Limited Liability Company)

Filing Fee: $100.00

TO: OKLAHOMA SECRETARY OF STATE
421 N.W. 13th, Suite 210
Oklahoma City, Oklahoma 73103
(405) 522-2520

I hereby execute the following articles of organization for the purpose of forming an Oklahoma limited liability company pursuant to the provisions of Title 18, Section 2005:

1. Name of the limited liability company: (**Note:** The name **shall** contain either the words **limited liability company** or **limited company** or the abbreviations **LLC, LC, L.L.C.** or **L.C.** The word **limited** may be abbreviated as **Ltd.**, and the word **company** may be abbreviated as **Co.**)

2. Street address of its principal place of business, wherever located:

| Street address | City | State | Zip Code |

(P.O. BOXES ARE **NOT** ACCEPTABLE)

3. **E-MAIL** address of the primary contact for the registered business:

❖ Notice of the Annual Certificate will **ONLY** be sent to the Limited Liability Company at its last known electronic mail address of record.

4. **NAME** and street address of the registered agent for service of process in the state of Oklahoma:

❖ The registered agent **shall** be the limited liability company itself, an individual resident of Oklahoma, **or** a domestic or qualified foreign corporation, limited liability company, or limited partnership.

Oklahoma

| Name | Street Address | City | State | Zip Code |

(P.O. BOXES ARE **NOT** ACCEPTABLE)

5. Term of existence:

❖ You may state **perpetual**, a set number of years, **or** a future effective expiration date. Perpetual means continuous.

The articles of organization **must** be signed by at least one (1) person who may or may not be a member of the limited liability company.

• Signature: _____ Dated: _____

• Printed Name: _____

(SOS FORM 0073-07/12)

76

WHAT'S KEEPING YOU FROM STARTING
THE BUSINESS GOD WANTS YOU TO HAVE?

PROCEDURES FOR ORGANIZING
AN OKLAHOMA PROFIT CORPORATION

This information is intended as an aid to organizing an Oklahoma profit corporation pursuant to the provisions of Title 18, Section 1001 of the Oklahoma Statutes. The Oklahoma General Corporation Act applies to all corporations except those expressly excluded and those for which special statutes are in existence with which the provisions of Title 18 may conflict. **PLEASE CONSULT THE STATUTES CAREFULLY.**

* It may be beneficial to contact the **INTERNAL REVENUE SERVICE** concerning federal tax requirements and the **OKLAHOMA TAX COMMISSION** concerning state tax requirements **prior to** filing with the Secretary of State.

FILING PROCEDURES:

1. Prepare and file with the Secretary of State one (1) signed copy of the certificate of incorporation.

2. Pay to the Secretary of State a **MINIMUM** filing fee of **Fifty Dollars ($50.00)**.

* The fee is one-tenth of one percent (1/10 of 1%) of the total authorized capital (TAC). The TAC is computed by multiplying the number of shares by the par value of each share. If the TAC is $50,000.00 or less, the filing fee is $50.00. If the TAC is greater than $50,000.00, the fee is $1.00 per $1,000.00. No par value stock is valued at **$50.00** per share for determining filing fees only. (Title 18, Section 1142)

3. Make checks, cashier's checks, or money orders payable to the Oklahoma Secretary of State. Instruments may be mailed, delivered in person, or filed on-line at www.sos.ok.gov. The address of the Secretary of State is 421 N.W. 13th, Suite 210, Oklahoma City, Oklahoma 73103. If delivered in person, there will be an additional Twenty- five Dollar ($25.00) fee for each document filed same day. The Secretary of State accepts Visa, Discover, MasterCard, or American Express if filing in person, or on-line; however, there will be a four percent (4%) service charge added for the use of a credit card. (Title 18, Section 1142).

INSTRUCTIONS FOR PREPARING THE CERTIFICATE OF INCORPORATION:

1. **NAME** – The name of the corporation which **SHALL** contain one of the words "association", "company", "corporation", "club", "foundation", "fund", "incorporated", "institute", "society", "union", "syndicate" or "limited" or one of the abbreviations "co.", "corp.", "inc.", "ltd.", or words or abbreviations of like import in other languages provided that such abbreviations are written in Roman characters or letters.

* The name shall be such as to distinguish it upon the records in the office of the Secretary of State from the names of: (1) corporations, both domestic and foreign, then existing or which have existed at any time during the preceding three (3) years; or (2) then existing domestic and foreign limited partnerships:

(SOS FORM 0001-07/12)

77

or (3) then existing domestic and foreign limited liability companies; or (4) trade names or fictitious names; or (5) corporate, limited partnership or limited liability company names reserved with the Secretary of State. (Title 18, Section 1006)

* The **AVAILABILITY** of a name can be checked in advance by telephoning the Secretary of State at **(405) 522-2520**, checking on-line at www.sos.ok.gov, or by coming in person. Prior to organizing a corporation, a name may be **reserved** for a period of **sixty (60) days** by filing a Name Reservation application and paying a **fee** of **Ten Dollars ($10.00)**. (Title 18, Section 1139)

2. **REGISTERED AGENT AND REGISTERED OFFICE** – The name and street address of the registered agent in the state of **Oklahoma**. The registered agent accepts service of process in the event of a lawsuit against the corporation. **Every** corporation **must** maintain a registered office and a registered agent. The agent may be the domestic corporation itself, an individual resident of this state, **or** a domestic or qualified foreign corporation, limited liability company, or limited partnership. Each registered agent shall maintain a business office identical with the registered office which is open during regular business hours to accept service of process and otherwise perform the functions of a registered agent. (Title 18, Sections 1021 & 1022) The registered office address must be a physical address and cannot be a post office address.

3. **E-MAIL ADDRESS** – The e-mail address of the primary contact for the registered business.

4. **DURATION** – The duration is the life span of the corporation. All domestic corporations shall have a perpetual duration unless otherwise stated. Perpetual means continuous.

5. **NATURE OF THE BUSINESS OR PURPOSE** – The purpose of the corporation is the type of business the corporation intends to conduct or promote. It shall be sufficient to state, either alone or with other business purposes, that the purpose of the corporation is **to engage in any lawful act or activity for which corporations may be organized under the general corporation law of Oklahoma.**

6. **AUTHORIZED CAPITAL (SHARES & PAR VALUE)** – Every business corporation **must** have authorized capital consisting of shares of stock and par value. The par value is the value assigned to each share. The total number of shares of stock, the designation of each class and series (if any) and the par value of the shares of each class and/or series of stock must be stated within the certificate of incorporation. Some classes include, but are not limited to, **COMMON STOCK** and **PREFERRED STOCK**. A definition of **Common Stock** and **Preferred Stock** may be found in a dictionary.

7. **INCORPORATORS** – A minimum of one (1) incorporator is required for organizing a profit corporation. **The incorporators are the original signers of the certificate of incorporation.** Any person, partnership, association or corporation, singly or jointly with others, and without regard to his or their residence, domicile or state of incorporation, may incorporate or organize a corporation pursuant to the provisions of the Oklahoma General Corporation Act. The incorporators are not necessarily officers, directors or shareholders, although it does not exclude them from being such. (Title 18, Section 1005)

8. **DIRECTORS** – If the powers of the incorporator or incorporators are to terminate upon the filing of the certificate of incorporation, the names and mailing addresses of the persons who are to serve as directors until the first annual meeting of shareholders or until their successors are elected and qualify.

9. **EXECUTION** – The certificate of incorporation shall be executed by the incorporator or incorporators. (Title 18, Section 1007)

(SOS FORM 0002-07/12)

WHAT'S KEEPING YOU FROM STARTING
THE BUSINESS GOD WANTS YOU TO HAVE?

CERTIFICATE OF INCORPORATION
(Oklahoma Corporation)

Filing Fee: Minimum $50.00

TO: OKLAHOMA SECRETARY OF STATE
421 N.W. 13th, Suite 210
Oklahoma City, Oklahoma 73103
(405) 522-2520

PLEASE NOTE:

* The **filing fee** is a **MINIMUM** of **$50.00**. The fee is one-tenth of one percent (1/10 or 1%) or $1.00 per $1,000.00 of the Total Authorized Capital (TAC). The TAC is computed by multiplying the number of shares by the par value of each share. If the TAC is $50,000 or less, the filing fee is $50.00. No par value stock is valued at $50.00.

I hereby execute the following articles for the purpose of forming an Oklahoma profit corporation pursuant to the provisions of Title 18, Section 1006:

1. Name of the corporation: (**Note:** The name of the corporation **shall** contain one of the words **association, company, corporation, club, foundation, fund, incorporated, institute, society, union, syndicate, limited** or any abbreviations thereof, with or without punctuation, which shall be such as to distinguish it upon the records in the Office of the Secretary of State.)

_____

2. **NAME** and street address of the registered agent for service of process in the state of Oklahoma:

   * The registered agent **shall** be the corporation itself, an individual resident of Oklahoma, **or** a domestic or qualified corporation, limited liability company, or limited partnership.

_____Oklahoma_____

| Name | Street Address (P.O. BOXES ARE **NOT** ACCEPTABLE) | City | State | Zip Code | County |

3. **E-MAIL** address of the primary contact for the registered business:

_____

4. Duration of the corporation is **perpetual**, unless otherwise stated: _____

5. Nature of the business or purposes for which the corporation is being formed:

   * It shall be sufficient to state, either alone or with other businesses or purposes, that the purpose of the corporation is to **engage in any lawful act or activity for which corporations may be organized under the general corporation law of Oklahoma.**

(SOS FORM 0002-07/12)

79

6. Total number of shares which the corporation shall have the authority to issue, designation of each class and each series, if any, and par value of the shares of each class and/or series:

* The par value per share is a dollar ($) amount and is also used for the calculation of the total filing fee.

CLASS	NUMBER OF SHARES	SERIES (If any)	PAR VALUE PER SHARE (Or, if without par value, so state)
COMMON			
PREFERRED			

7. Name and mailing address of the undersigned incorporator(s):

* There must be at least one (1) incorporator.

NAME	MAILING ADDRESS	CITY	STATE	ZIP CODE

8. If the powers of the incorporator(s) are to terminate upon the filing of the certificate of incorporation, the name and mailing address of the person(s) who are to serve as director(s):

NAME	MAILING ADDRESS	CITY	STATE	ZIP CODE

The certificate of incorporation **must** be signed by all **incorporators** stated within article #7.

- Signature of Incorporator: _____ Dated: _____

- Signature of Incorporator: _____ Dated: _____

(SOS FORM 0002-07/12)

WHAT'S KEEPING YOU FROM STARTING
THE BUSINESS GOD WANTS YOU TO HAVE?

PROCEDURES FOR ORGANIZING
AN OKLAHOMA NOT FOR PROFIT CORPORATION

This information is intended as an aid to organizing an Oklahoma not for profit corporation pursuant to the provisions of Title 18, Section 1001 of the Oklahoma Statutes. **PLEASE CONSULT THE STATUTES CAREFULLY.**

❖ It may be to your benefit to contact the **INTERNAL REVENUE SERVICE** concerning federal tax requirements and the **OKLAHOMA TAX COMMISSION** concerning state tax requirements **prior to** filing with the Secretary of State.

FILING PROCEDURES:

1. **Prepare** and file with the Secretary of State one (1) signed copy of the certificate of incorporation.

2. **Pay** to the Secretary of State a **filing fee** of **Twenty-five Dollars ($25.00).** (Title 18, Section 1142)

3. Make checks, cashier's checks, or money orders payable to the Oklahoma Secretary of State. Instruments may be mailed, delivered in person, or filed on-line at www.sos.ok.gov. The address of the Secretary of State is 421 N.W. 13th, Suite 210, Oklahoma City, Oklahoma 73103. If delivered in person, there will be an additional Twenty-five Dollar ($25.00) fee for each document filed same day. The Secretary of State accepts Visa, Discover, MasterCard, or American Express if filing in person, or on-line; however, there will be a four percent (4%) service charge added for the use of a credit card. (Title 18, Section 1142)

INSTRUCTIONS FOR PREPARING THE CERTIFICATE OF INCORPORATION:

1. **NAME** – The name of the corporation which **SHALL** contain one of the words "association", "company", "corporation", "club", "foundation", "fund", "incorporated", "institute", "society", "union", "syndicate", "limited" or one of the abbreviations "co.", "corp.", "inc.", "ltd.", or words or abbreviations of like import in other languages provided that such abbreviations are written in Roman characters or letters.

❖ The name shall be such as to distinguish it upon the records in the office of the Secretary of State from the names of: (1) corporations, both domestic and foreign, then existing or which have existed at any time during the preceding three (3) years; or (2) then existing domestic and foreign limited partnerships; or (3) then existing domestic and foreign limited liability companies; or (4) trade names or fictitious names; or (5) corporate, limited partnership or limited liability company names reserved with the Secretary of State. (Title 18, Section 1006)

❖ The **AVAILABILITY** of a name can be checked in advance by telephoning the Secretary of State at **(405) 522-2520,** checking on-line at www.sos.ok.gov, or by coming in person. Prior to organizing a corporation, a name may be **reserved** for a period of **sixty (60) days** by filing a Name Reservation application and paying a fee of **Ten Dollars ($10.00).** (Title 18, Section 1139)

(SOS FORM 0008-07/12)

2. **REGISTERED AGENT AND REGISTERED OFFICE** – The name and street address of the registered agent in the state of Oklahoma. The registered agent accepts service of process in the event of a lawsuit against the corporation. **Every** corporation **must** maintain a registered office and a registered agent in the state of Oklahoma. The agent may be the corporation itself, an individual resident of this state, **or** a domestic or qualified foreign corporation, limited liability company, or limited partnership. Each registered agent shall maintain a business office identical with the registered office which is open during regular business hours to accept service of process and otherwise perform the functions of a registered agent. (Title 18, Sections 1021 & 1022) The registered office address must be a physical address and cannot be a post office address.

3. **LOCATION OF CHURCH** – In the event the corporation is a church, the street address of the location of the church must be included within the certificate of incorporation. The address of the church must be a street address and cannot be a post office box address. Rural routes and box numbers are acceptable. An address is not required if the corporation is not a church.

4. **DURATION** – The duration of the corporation is the life span of the corporation. All domestic corporations shall have a perpetual duration unless otherwise stated. Perpetual means continuous.

5. **NATURE OF THE BUSINESS OR PURPOSE** – The purpose of the corporation is the type of business the corporation intends to conduct or promote. It shall be sufficient to state, either alone or with other purposes, that the purpose of the corporation is **to engage in any lawful act or activity for which corporations may be organized under the general corporation law of Oklahoma**, and by such statement all lawful acts and activities shall be within the purposes of the corporation, except for express limitations, if any.

6. This language is required to be stated within the certificate of incorporation. This statement does not require an answer when completing the form.

7. This language is required to be stated within the certificate of incorporation. This statement does not require an answer when completing the form.

8. **NUMBER OF TRUSTEES/DIRECTORS** – The number of trustees or directors to be elected at the first meeting of the corporation.

9. **TRUSTEES/DIRECTORS** – A minimum of **ONE (1)** trustee or director is required. The name and mailing address of each trustee or director must be included within the certificate of incorporation.

10. **INCORPORATORS** – A minimum of **THREE (3)** incorporators is required to form a not for profit corporation. **The incorporators are the original signers of the certificate of incorporation.** Any person, partnership, association, or corporation, singly or jointly with others, and without regard to his or their residence, domicile or state of incorporation, may incorporate or organize a corporation pursuant to the provisions of the Oklahoma General Corporation Act. The incorporators are not necessarily officers, directors or shareholders, although it does not exclude them from being such. (Title 18, Section 1005)

11. **E-MAIL ADDRESS** – The e-mail address of the primary contact for the registered business.

12. **EXECUTION** – The certificate of incorporation shall be executed by the incorporator or incorporators. (Title 18, Section 1007)

(SOS FORM 0008-07/12)

82

WHAT'S KEEPING YOU FROM STARTING
THE BUSINESS GOD WANTS YOU TO HAVE?

CERTIFICATE OF INCORPORATION
(Oklahoma Not for Profit Corporation)

Filing Fee $25.00

TO: OKLAHOMA SECRETARY OF STATE
421 N.W. 13th, Suite 210
Oklahoma City, Oklahoma 73103
(405) 522-2520

I hereby execute the following articles for the purpose of forming an Oklahoma not for profit corporation pursuant to the provisions of Title 18, Section 1006:

1. Name of the corporation: (**Note**: The name of the corporation **shall** contain one of the words **association, company, corporation, club, foundation, fund, incorporated, institute, society, union, syndicate, limited** or any abbreviations thereof, with or without punctuation, which shall be such as to distinguish it upon the records in the Office of the Secretary of State.)

2. **NAME** and the street address of the registered agent for service of process in the State of Oklahoma:

   ❖ The registered agent **shall** be the corporation itself, an individual resident of Oklahoma, **or** a domestic or qualified foreign corporation, limited liability company, or limited partnership.

Name	Street Address (P.O. BOXES ARE **NOT** ACCEPTABLE)	City	State	Zip Code	County
			Oklahoma		

3. In the event the corporation is a **CHURCH**, the street address of its location in Oklahoma:

Street Address (P.O. BOXES ARE **NOT** ACCEPTABLE)	City	State	Zip Code
		Oklahoma	

4. Duration of the corporation is perpetual, unless otherwise stated: _____

5. Nature of the business or purposes for which the corporation is being formed:

   ❖ It shall be sufficient to state, either alone or with other businesses or purposes, that the purpose of the corporation is to **engage in any lawful act or activity for which corporations may be organized under the general corporation law of Oklahoma.**

(SOS FORM 0009-07/12)

6. This corporation does not have authority to issue capital stock.

7. This corporation is not for profit, and as such the corporation does not afford pecuniary gain, incidentally or otherwise, to its members.

8. Number of trustees or directors to be elected at the first meeting: _____
   ❖ There must be at least **one** (1) trustee or director elected.

9. Names and mailing addresses of each person who will serve as a trustee or director:
   ❖ There must be at least **one** (1) trustee or director.

Name	Mailing Address	City	State	Zip Code

10. Names and mailing addresses of the **undersigned incorporators**:
    ❖ There must be at least **three** (3) incorporators.

Name	Mailing Address	City	State	Zip Code

11. **E-MAIL** address of the primary contact for the registered business:

_____

The certificate of incorporation must be signed by all incorporators stated within article #10.

- Signature of Incorporator: _____ Dated: _____

- Signature of Incorporator: _____ Dated: _____

- Signature of Incorporator: _____ Dated: _____

WHAT'S KEEPING YOU FROM STARTING
THE BUSINESS GOD WANTS YOU TO HAVE?

40001
OKLAHOMA BUSINESS REGISTRATION APPLICATION

Business Name: _____   FEIN/SSN: _____

Section 1 Indicate the reason(s) for filing this form:

A ☐ New Business

B ☐ Additional License/Permit

C ☐ Other (explain)

Section 2 Contact Information:

1. **Business Phone** (_____) _____   **Business Fax** (_____) _____

   Name _____   Email Address _____

Section 3 Ownership Type:

2. How is this business owned?

   A ☐ Individual (Sole Proprietor)   B ☐ General Partnership   C ☐ Limited Partnership

   D ☐ Oklahoma Corporation   E ☐ Foreign Corporation   F ☐ Limited Liability Company

   G ☐ Other (explain) _____

3. **Federal Employer's Identification Number (FEIN)** ☐☐ - ☐☐☐☐☐☐☐

4. **Name of Individual, Partnership, Corporation, Limited Liability Company or Other**

   _____

   Social Security Number, if Individual ☐☐☐ - ☐☐ - ☐☐☐☐

   Mailing Address _____

   City _____ State _____ Zip _____ County _____

5. **Names of Partners/Responsible Corporate Officers/Managing Members:** See instructions.
   (If Social Security Number is not provided below, the application will be returned for completion.)

A {
First Name	Middle Initial	Last Name		Social Security Number	Title	
Mailing Address			City		State	Zip Code

B {
First Name	Middle Initial	Last Name		Social Security Number	Title	
Mailing Address			City		State	Zip Code

C {
First Name	Middle Initial	Last Name		Social Security Number	Title	
Mailing Address			City		State	Zip Code

A
Application continued on page B...

40001

OKLAHOMA BUSINESS REGISTRATION APPLICATION

Business Name: _____ FEIN/SSN: _____

Section 5 (continued)

For multiple locations, indicate the number of copies attached: _____

18. Is this a home based business? (see instructions).. ☐ Yes ☐ No

19. Was there a previous business at this location? (if yes, complete questions 20 and 21)... ☐ Yes ☐ No

20. If you answered yes on question 19, please provide the following information:

_____ _____ _____
Previous Owner's Permit Number   Name   Phone Number

_____ _____ _____
Physical Address   City   State   Zip

21. If you answered yes on question 19, are you using tangible items owned by the previous business owner? (i.e. fixtures and/or equipment; items for resale - this does not include real property).. ☐ Yes ☐ No

22. If you answered yes on question 21, did you pay sales tax on the tangible items purchased for use from the previous business owner? (i.e. fixtures and/or equipment; items for resale - this does not include real property) .... ☐ Yes ☐ No

Section 6 Sales and Use Tax

23. If you currently hold or have previously held an Oklahoma Sales Tax Permit and/or Oklahoma Use Tax Permit, list number(s):

Sales Tax: _____	Use Tax: _____
Sales Tax: _____	Use Tax: _____
Sales Tax: _____	Use Tax: _____
Sales Tax: _____	Use Tax: _____

24. Date of first sales subject to sales and/or use tax in Oklahoma.......(month/day/year) ___/___/___

25. Date of first sales, if applicable, subject to mixed beverage gross receipts tax ....(month/day/year) ___/___/___

26. Do you make purchases from outside Oklahoma that are for your company's consumption or use in Oklahoma, and are not for resale on which tax is owed? (see instructions on page 7)... ☐ Yes ☐ No

If you are an out-of-state business, please complete lines 27-28.

27. (a) Do you maintain an inventory for sale in Oklahoma?.................................... ☐ Yes ☐ No

(b) Do you lease goods/equipment in Oklahoma?... ☐ Yes ☐ No

28. How are your goods delivered in Oklahoma?

☐ Common Carrier ☐ Own Vehicles ☐ Both (Common Carrier and Own Vehicles)

29. Do you sell and install or contract for the installation of equipment in Oklahoma? .... ☐ Yes ☐ No

See page 10 for reporting requirements.

C

Application continued on page D.

40001

OKLAHOMA BUSINESS REGISTRATION LICENSE AND FEES

Business Name: _____ FEIN/SSN: _____

Mailing Address: _____

City: _____ State: _____ Zip: _____ County: _____

Notice : All registrations and license fees must be paid with the Business Registration Application. Failure to include the fees will delay processing of your application. Refer to the "Instructions and Definitions" pages within this packet for further information regarding fees.

Please check (✓) the appropriate box(es) for each license and/or permit that you are applying for and enter the applicable fee amount in the "Total" column at the far right.

License or Permit Type	Basic Fee (each)	Tax Code	Total
☐ 1. **Sales Tax Permit (retail and wholesale)**........$ 20.00		SLP....$ _____.00 ⌐	
☐ 2. **Sales Tax Permit for Additional Locations**			SLP Subtotal
(Number of Locations _____)... @$ 10.00		SLP....$ _____.00	$ _____.00
☐ 3. **Wholesale Low Point Beer**			
(3.2 Beer) License.....................$ 250.00		ALP....$ _____.00 ⌐	
☐ 4. **Manufacturer Low Point Beer**			ALP Subtotal
(3.2 Beer) License......................$ 500.00		ALP....$ _____.00	$ _____.00
☐ 5. **Retailer Manufacturer Low Point Beer**			
(Brew Pub) License....................$ 650.00		SLP....$ _____.00 ⌐	
☐ 6. **Retail Dealer for Low Point Beer (3.2 Beer) License Fees:**			
Draught, Bottle and Can License			
(on-premise consumption)...............$ 500.00		SLP....$ _____.00	
Bottle and Can Only License			
(on-premise consumption)...............$ 350.00		SLP....$ _____.00	
Off Premise.........................$ 230.00		SLP....$ _____.00	SLP Subtotal
Special Event Fee			
(per day: __ / __ / ___ to __ / __ / __ $ 5.00		SLP....$ _____.00	$ _____.00
☐ 7. **Cash Bond for** _____ **Tax** ------		CSF ...$ _____.00	$ _____.00
☐ 8. **Coin-Operated Device Distributor Permit**.....$ 200.00		COP............................	$ _____.00
Make Checks Payable to: Oklahoma Tax Commission. TOTAL AMOUNT DUE..................			$ _____.00

E

Form G-900
Revised 5-2016

AFFIDAVIT VERIFYING LAWFUL
PRESENCE IN THE UNITED STATES

All sole proprietors applying for a business permit or license with the Oklahoma Tax Commission are required, by the provisions of 56 O.S. Supp 2007 Section 71, to provide the Commission with verification of lawful presence in the United States by executing the Affidavit below before a notary public or other officer authorized to notarize affidavits under State law.

➤ **This affidavit must be returned with your license/permit application.**

State of Oklahoma

County of: _____

I, _____ being of lawful age, state under penalty
print name
of perjury, as follows:

Please check the appropriate box(es)

☐ My Social Security Number is: _____

☐ My Individual Tax Identification Number is: _____

☐ I am a United States Citizen.

☐ I am a qualified alien under the Federal Immigration and Nationality Act and am lawfully present in the United States.
My Alien Registration Number (A#) or I-94 Number is: * _____

Date of Birth: * _____

I state under penalty of perjury under the laws of Oklahoma the foregoing is true and correct and I have read and understand this form and executed it in my own hand.

Signature of Applicant _____

Subscribed and sworn to or affirmed before me this _____ day of _____, 20_____ ,

by _____ (applicant name - please print).

Notary: _____

My Commission Expires: _____

My Commission Number: _____

*Either the A# or the I-94 number, and date of birth must be provided. The Alien Registration Number (A#) and the I-94 (arrival/departure) numbers are issued by the U.S. Citizenship and Immigration Service.

Official Use Only:		
Homeland Security Verified: _____	Date: _____	Initials: ____
OTC Signature Witness: _____	Date: _____	

F

88

NOTES

Chapter 1: Creating the Vision

1. *BibleGateway.com: A searchable online Bible in over 150 versions and 50 languages.*, www.biblegateway.com.

2. *Entrepreneur,* www.entrepreneur.com

3. *OpenBibleinfo.,* www.openbibleinfo.com.

4. Oxford Pocket English Dictionary. Oxford University Press, 2008.

Chapter 2: Developing the Entrepreneur in You

1. *BibleGateway.com: A searchable online Bible in over 150 versions and 50 languages.*, www.biblegateway.com.

2. *BusinessDictionary.,* www.businessdictionary.com

3. *Chron.,* www.smallbusiness.chron.com

4. *Forbes.,* www.forbes.com

5. *OpenBibleinfo.,* www.openbibleinfo.com.

6. Oxford Pocket English Dictionary. Oxford University Press, 2008.

Chapter 3: of a Great Leader: Seeking the Eagle Inside You

1. *BibleGateway.com: A searchable online Bible in over 150 versions and 50 languages.*, www.biblegateway.com.

2. *Entrepreneur,* www.entrepreneur.com

3. *OpenBibleinfo.,* www.openbibleinfo.com.

4. Oxford Pocket English Dictionary. Oxford

University Press, 2008.

Chapter 4: Process of Seed, Time, and Harvest

1. *BibleGateway.com: A searchable online Bible in over 150 versions and 50 languages.*, www.biblegateway.com.

2. *OpenBibleinfo.*, www.openbibleinfo.com.

3. Oxford Pocket English Dictionary. Oxford University Press, 2008.

Chapter 5: Obedience, Consistency, and Persistence

1. BibleGateway." BibleGateway.com: A searchable online Bible in over 150 versions and 50 languages., www.biblegateway.com/.

Chapter 6 : Entrepreneurs Instinct

1. Oxford Pocket English Dictionary. Oxford University Press, 2008.

Chapter 7: Don't Stop, Keep Going, and Stand on God's Word: Overcoming Trails and Tribulations

1. *BibleGateway.com: A searchable online Bible in over 150 versions and 50 languages.*, www.biblegateway.com.

2. *OpenBibleinfo.*, www.openbibleinfo.com.

Chapter 8: Your Start-up Guide for the Business that Awaits

1. "How to Start a Business." *Oklahoma Department of Commerce*, okcommerce.gov/business/startup/.

WHAT'S KEEPING YOU FROM STARTING
THE BUSINESS GOD WANTS YOU TO HAVE?

Chapter 9: Are You Ready? Let's Create The Master Plan

1. *Entrepreneur,* www.entrepreneur.com

Chapter 10: Resources for your Business

1. IRS - state government websites at www.irs.gov/businesses/small-businesses-self-employed/state-government-websites
2. Oklahoma Secretary of State - *Business Forms,* www.sos.ok.gov/business/forms.aspx.